FROM THE DIARY OF MADAME MAO

CMUP Literary Translation
Nicky Agate and Jake Grefenstette, Series Editors

Also by María Teresa Ogliastri

Cola de plata
Nosotros los inmortales
Polo sur
Del diario de la señora Mao
Bendito verdor

Also translated by Yvette Neisser & Patricia Bejarano Fisher

South Pole / Polo Sur, by María Teresa Ogliastri

FROM THE DIARY OF MADAME MAO

by

MARÍA TERESA OGLIASTRI

translated by

YVETTE NEISSER

&

PATRICIA BEJARANO FISHER

Carnegie Mellon University Press
Pittsburgh 2026

Acknowledgments

Grateful acknowledgment is made to the editors of the publications where the English translations of the following poems first appeared, sometimes in earlier versions:

The Adirondack Review: "A Thousand Cranes," "Colors of Violence," "Return to the Countryside," "From a Chinese Legend," and "Speak to Me Tree"
Beltway Poetry Quarterly: "Outside a Frog Is Croaking" and "Rain"
Blue Lyra Review: "Alfalfa Sprouts" and "To Be Empress"
Duende: "Since Then I Have No Mercy" and "*The Sleeping Beauty*"
Eleven Eleven: "On How I Became a Wife," "My Entertainment," "The Chill of Siberia," "Temple," and "Bonsai"
Lunch Ticket: "Just Following Orders," "If You Raise Crows," and "My Daughter Na's Visit"
Mid-Atlantic Review: "Lark Please Look at Me"
Vox Populi: "Omen," "Five Flower Lake," "Teach Me Tree"
Zone 3: "Lotus Feet" and "Red Guards"

The introductory essay, "Female Power: the Silkworm's Prison" by Ana María Velázquez Anderson, was originally published in Spanish in the Venezuelan newspaper *El Nacional* on December 1, 2013.

Book design by Connie Amoroso

Library of Congress Control Number 2026937116
ISBN 978-0-88748-746-0

Printed and bound in the United States of America

10 9 8 7 6 5 4 3 2 1

CONTENTS

FEMALE POWER: THE SILKWORM'S PRISON

Writing about Madame Mao is a difficult task for a female poet. Nothing is farther from creativity than power. However, Maria Teresa Ogliastri accepted the challenge, becoming one of the few women writers in Venezuela to have addressed this topic. Obviously, feelings of rejection arose spontaneously when faced with the terrible figure of Jiang Qing (1914–1991), the fourth wife of Mao Zedong (1893–1976). This woman, at the head of the Ministry of Culture, along with the rest of "The Gang of Four," led the so-called "Great Proletarian Cultural Revolution" (1966–1976), a state-run wave of sustained political violence that imprisoned, tortured, and assassinated thousands of intellectuals, artists, and academics accused of being "bourgeois" or "revisionists," or simply because Madame Mao considered them potential threats against her or her husband. It is estimated that in just one year, 500,000 intellectuals were executed—with China losing the majority of its intellegentsia.

Ogliastri moves between the boundaries of historic reality and fiction. Her collection of poems is presented as entries in a fictional diary, whose pages, she says, "came to me in a beautiful disarray like fall leaves scattered by wind." Thus, the poet separates her voice from a story which is not hers, which belongs in its entirety to Madame Mao.

But doubt appears. The poet stops at the apex of horror, but rises above it in order to understand the reason for that ambition. By way of explanation, the author describes her moral stance when writing about Madame Mao: "I was overcome by conflicting feelings." She believes that power is an illness of the soul, adding, "To face these totalitarian entities, one must understand why they lost their humanity."

Ogliastri explores, searches, and ponders the source of a woman's attraction to power. She takes the reader to Madame Mao's childhood, to a life of poverty in a home with a violent father, to poorly bound feet that instead of beauty brought pain and ended up "gnarled like an old tree." She goes on to give voice to the beautiful young woman who loved the theater and, abandoned by a first husband, throws herself into adventure, fully aware that she has the feminine strength needed to take a "tiger's leap in the brush," a metaphor for her opportunism in the search for power. Subsequently, the poet outlines Jiang Qing's failure with a second husband, and then goes on to the complexity of her self-serving surrender to love with Mao Zedong, a married man twenty-one years her elder. While he devoted himself to high government, she was training the Red Guard for citizen repression. The poet closes by imagining Madame Mao's last days alone and desperate in a jail cell, awaiting execution.

The writing flows from the nothingness of a jail cell with nothing but a light bulb hanging from the ceiling and a cot. Jiang Qing was imprisoned as soon as her husband died in 1976, was tried, and was condemned to death. Her last days were spent in a cell, watching a silkworm devour its leaves in its wooden box, a metaphor for her own situation. Earlier, in a historic trial, she had become desperate and yelled at her judges, trying to justify the unjustifiable when the blood of her opponents was still fresh on her hands. Later, in the clarity of her last moments, when she already felt the rope approaching her neck, she asked for help, but everyone turned their back on her.

Power, a Woman's Prison

In reality, since early in life, Madame Mao "imprisons herself" in a psychological jail that keeps her from fully exercising her freedom as a woman. She is drawn to power—not the way women naturally are toward maternal authority, which is theirs and which stems from the possibility of motherhood, and which is wielded primarily over children—but rather toward a masculine form of power that forces her to submit to the dictates of the patriarchy. The patriarchy grants her a certain amount of power but reserves control for itself. Once used, a woman is discarded, just like the silkworm when it stops making its precious product.

Power in the female sphere translates into life in prison. Just like the silkworm, Madame Mao has lost her natural habitat. She does not need the forest or the light, says the poet. Her wooden box is her enslavement. Power is patriarchal and masculine, authority is feminine. Seeking power entails forgetting herself: "to achieve obedience / I covered my head with a tortoise shell / for thirty years." Neither forest nor light, because the confinement of power impedes the natural growth associated with the forest and the mental clarity associated with light.

The Ascent

The slope is steep, the ascent somber. Madame Mao knows this: "the taller the tree / the longer its shadow." Moreover, what's important is not only to climb, but to remain at the top, come what may. When she learned that Mao Zedong was approaching the city with his warriors, she went out to meet him. She became his lover in the caves where the revolutionaries were hiding in the mountainous region of Jiangxi. While Mao Zedong, unquestioned leader of sharp intelligence, but with a complex private life, held complete dominance over the citizenry, she was offered the exercise of crime: "it wasn't easy living in a cave / but the dragon said / stone by stone you have torn down my cities / would you like to crush heads?"

Ogliastri points out Madame Mao's guilt and her grave mistake. From her prison, the author forces her to reflect on her past, when she was known as "the white-boned demon," a woman absolutely faithful to her husband and his cause, without regard for morality: "my loyalty proved me a hyena / if he said attack / I attacked / the army was my dagger / I was my master's dog / his bone / his dark side."

In the poem "Colors of Violence," there is a visceral reaction against her opponents: "they still dared / to write against me // in the Great Hall of the People / I took out paintbrushes / placed bowls for water on the table // nothing like blood for painting azaleas." Violence is depicted as a fundamental aspect of power, a restrained violence that rekindles with each instance of contempt, and when it finally emerges, it does so in an explosion of cruelty.

Just Following Orders

Madame Mao despairs in her prison. She recriminates and manipulates her only daughter: "why are you ashamed of me? / a widow is a bird with just one wing // when you come to say goodbye bring cellophane / to wrap my heart tender and throbbing." Her daughter turns her back on her. So her attention turns to elements of nature to which she bestows the power to help her: she asks the tree to speak to her, to give her patience, she asks the lark to look her in the eye to conjure death. Then she turns her gaze towards her body, the last refuge. In the loneliness of her cell comes acceptance of the void: "Body get used to this / ceilings white as wax / where flocks of birds crash / into the void."

In "Just Following Orders," she wields the typical excuse of those who commit genocide: "there are circumstances / just following orders." The cot full of bedbugs, the cold, the bitterness of knowing she's not loved by the people make her reflect: "the ingratitude of the masses / is opaque glass." Consciousness weighs with clarity. Her fatal destiny appears before her: execution or, with luck, suicide, the same end as those she persecuted.

In the end, the poet's voice asserts itself, insisting on the reintegration of the human, which only poetry and literature can provide. The story of Madame Mao must be understood so that cruelty will not occur on its own without intervening circumstances, so that evil will not triumph, so that the eternal promise of regeneration will remain intact.

—Ana María Velázquez Anderson
Universidad Metropolitana
Venezuela

NOTE: In 1991, after fifteen years in prison, Jiang Qing was released from prison due to pressure from international human rights NGOs because she was suffering from throat cancer. The Chinese government stated that she died by suicide ten days after leaving prison.

MADAME MAO: POWER AS AN ILLNESS OF THE SOUL

The purpose of these lines is to tell of the moral scruples and the political intent that took shape during the creative process that brought about this book, *From the Diary of Madame Mao*. I wanted to reach a deep understanding of the soul of Jiang Qing, the fourth wife of Mao Zedong, who took part in a form of absolute, tyrannical power. While writing this book, I was overcome by conflicting feelings. At times I felt scruples in presenting Madame Mao in such a kind way. I realize now that this fictional diary shows the mental illness of a character who shares a kinship of evil with Lady Macbeth. To face these totalitarian entities, one must understand why they lost their humanity.

Madame Mao is ill. Her guilt burdens her. But she cannot cope with that guilt. She cannot find redemption. Hence her madness. Tyrants try to silence the voice of their conscience. They choose madness rather than confronting the truth. I have opted for compassion. I firmly believe that the poetic image goes beyond ideological distortions and reveals true humanity. My hope is that this book will contribute to that awakening of the conscience. It does not pretend to be ideological. Nor is it my intention to issue a call to political action, what James Joyce called "pornography." Rather, it is an invitation to discover compassion toward this individual. She is part of me and part of us all—the part that is tempted by the abyss. I believe this is a higher form of politics. It is what Socrates was seeking when he shone his light on the citizens of the polis. Poetry must be true and must move the reader. Moving the reader means, as William Blake said, purifying "the doors of perception," lifting the blinds of ideology. Poetry is not indifferent to the polis; on the contrary, it is destined to offer it the most disinterested service. Poetry exists because it can redeem the polis and thus free the human soul from the sickness of power.

—María Teresa Ogliastri

TRANSLATORS' NOTE

María Teresa Ogliastri has long been a renowned Venezuelan poet, included in anthologies and poetry festivals across Latin America. A distinctive feature of her poetry is the proclivity to write in the voice of a character. For instance, her first book, *Cola de plata* (*Silver Tail*), is written from the perspective of a whale, and *Polo Sur* in the voice of her late father. A longtime resident of Caracas, she has lived through the tumultuous political and economic era of the Chavez regime (1999–2013) and the Maduro regime, which gave her a keen understanding of authoritarian figures and their impact on citizens' lives. Her sensitivity to all these aspects of the human and societal experience, coupled with her perspective as a philosopher, come to bear in the present collection (originally published in 2011, near the end of the Chavez regime).

We initially got to know Ogliastri's work in the late 2000s, when a mutual friend brought us a copy of her book, *Polo Sur*, a sequence of poems relating her father's imaginary journey from the Amazon jungle to the South Pole. We fell in love with her distinctive poetic voice and translated the book (*South Pole / Polo Sur*, published by Settlement House, 2011). When she told us that her next book of poems would tell the story of the Mao era in China through the voice of his wife, Jiang Qing, we were immediately eager to translate it.

From the Diary of Madame Mao emerged from Ogliastri's extensive research into the lives of both Jiang Qing and Mao, as well as Chinese history, culture, and literature. Thus, before we could embark on the translation, we had to become familiar with the subject matter. We believe that translating poetry requires the translator to "become" the author, as we are tasked with writing the poems in a new language. So we started out by reading a biography of Jiang Qing (*Madame Mao: The White-Boned Demon*, by Ross Terrill), as well as a historical novel (*Becoming Madame Mao*, by Anchee Min), recommended by Ogliastri.

Because of the multilayered nature of the project—where the language is Spanish, but all the cultural references are Chinese—the translation process was also multilayered. First, we applied the collaborative process that we had developed in translating *South Pole*, which involves "identifying the essential elements" of the author's style so that we can maintain consistency in the voice of the translations, regardless of who is working on a particular poem. For Ogliastri, the key elements are concise language, using line or stanza breaks in lieu of punctuation, and a strong emphasis on imagery. In fact, with Ogliastri's poetry, the image often takes precedence over the words, so that the process requires translating image by image rather than line by line.

The second, added layer in the translation process involved researching the historical, biographical, or cultural references to ensure that we were representing these accurately and using the appropriate English terminology. An example is the first line of "My Daughter Na's Visit," which literally could be translated, "There was a time when I loved beyond pain/hurt." But we knew from our reading that Jiang Qing's childhood had been traumatic and involved a great deal of suffering: poverty, domestic violence, social humiliation, and then abandonment by her mother. Thus, we decided that Ogliastri's *dolor* would best be captured by "suffering" and that *más allá* in this case implied depth of emotion and passion rather than distance, hence we chose "deeper" rather than the standard translation "beyond."

While we each brought our respective expertise to the project—Patricia as "the Spanish linguist" and Yvette as "the poet"—we collaborated equally on all aspects of the translation process. We divided the poems, each of us producing a first draft of half of the poems. Then we came together, in many delightful sessions, to review, discuss, and revise the translations, often diving into our big pile of reference books for ideas and clarifications: Spanish and English monolingual dictionaries, a bilingual dictionary, a thesaurus, and Jiang Qing's biography.

We also benefited greatly from consulting directly with the author. As we worked through the poems, we compiled queries about particular lines, images, or historical and biographical references we were unsure of, and sent these to Ogliastri, who always responded thoughtfully and in detail. Understanding her thinking behind each of the poems, as well as the book as a whole, helped us to ensure that the translations capture Ogliastri's poetic intent.

We hope that this bilingual edition will bring further attention to Ogliastri's poetry among English-language readership, as well as shed new light on the history of Mao-era China from a twenty-first-century Latin American perspective. One history illuminates another.

—Yvette Neisser & Patricia Bejarano Fisher
Silver Spring, Maryland, August 2025

Perhaps women were once so dangerous
that they had to have their feet bound.

—Maxine Hong Kingston

I don't know any relationship other than inequality
and I can attest that sex is engaging
in the first rounds,
but what sustains interest
in the long run
is power

—Jiang Qing

For a long time, these poems were in a chest belonging to Madame Mao, left to the brutal devices of mice. They were rescued by a boy's hand while he was flying a kite. They came to me in a beautiful disarray like fall leaves scattered by wind.

DESDE ENTONCES NO CONOZCO LA PIEDAD

Sentí el piquetazo

el dedo
inerme

petrificado
el cangrejo giraba los ojos

mi abuelo lo ensartó en un palo
para que perdiera el miedo

le dije   mátalo
la ira es un placer

bajo las vendas el odio nace con el sol

mi abuelo liberó al cangrejo que volvió a la arena
como si supiera que con mi dedo
taparía los orificios de las cuevas

desde entonces no conozco la piedad

SINCE THEN I HAVE NO MERCY

I felt the pinch

my toe
defenseless

petrified
the crab swiveled its eyes

my grandfather nailed it on a stick
so I could conquer fear

I said   kill it
wrath is a pleasure

under the bandages hate rises with the sun

my grandfather released the crab which returned to the sand
as if knowing that with my toe
I would seal the openings to its caves

since then I have no mercy

PIES DE LOTO

Mi madre aseguró
que vendar mis pies traería buena fortuna
y que pasado el dolor sería hermosa

esa mañana los pasteles de arroz
amanecieron intactos
los espíritus no vinieron

el vendaje fracasó y mis pies quedaron
torcidos como un árbol antiguo

el regreso de los cisnes salvajes no trajo mensaje alguno
¿seré emperatriz después de este dolor?

mi madre respondió
la mente del hombre es un caballo desbocado
déjalo correr sin bridas y será una montaña
si aprendes a someter tu voluntad
en primavera llegarás a esposa

ni esposa ni manceba
seré emperatriz de China
con súbditos y vasallos a mis pies
cien mil cabezas caerán a mi izquierda
y diez mil a mi derecha
y si mi mano temblara
la cortaré

LOTUS FEET

My mother promised
that binding my feet would bring good fortune
that after the pain I would be beautiful

next morning the rice cakes
remained untouched
the spirits hadn't come

the binding failed and my feet came out
gnarled like an old tree

the wild swans' return brought no message at all
will I be empress after this pain?

my mother responded
a man's mind is a runaway horse
let him run unbridled and he'll be a mountain
if you learn to subdue your will
come spring you'll be a wife

neither wife nor concubine
I will be empress of China
with subjects and servants at my feet
a hundred thousand heads will fall at my left
ten thousand at my right
and if my hand should tremble
I shall sever it

HADAS CAÍDAS

No puede ser una granja
un lugar donde habitan silfos y hadas

no venderé mi jardín de flores y pájaros

las gentecillas de las fuentes ya no cantan
sólo murmullos en el lago

en mi jardín
ya no hay ogros

sólo cantan mirlos

las doncellas están afuera
y es probable que vaguen en el bosque
por haber descuidado la virtud

bajo el puente una cabellera irisa el agua

varias doncellas atraviesan el lago
son las ninfas
las cautivas

ahora que el estanque está cubierto de lotos
sólo la castidad podrá salvarlas

FALLEN FAIRIES

A place inhabited by sylphs and fairies
cannot be just a farm

I will not sell my garden of flowers and birds

the figures in the fountains no longer sing
just murmurs in the lake

in my garden
there are no more ogres

only blackbirds sing

the maidens are outside
probably roaming the forest
for having neglected their virtue

under the bridge a woman's hair shimmers in the water

some maidens cross the lake
they are the nymphs
the captives

now that the pond is covered in lotus
only chastity can save them

BROTES DE ALFALFA

Mi madre era de bambú
cuando la brisa movía su falda
veía las marcas en sus piernas delgadas

mi padre tomaba la cintura de sauce
y la zarandeaba como una marioneta sin hilos

la última concubina
haría todo el trabajo de la casa
si no tenía un hijo varón

los pies de mi madre eran una carreta
andaban andaban andaban
sin cansarse

la recuerdo tumbada en la hierba
cerca de la pequeña alberca
donde nadaban los patos

con una jarrita de porcelana recogía agua
y me acercaba hasta donde ella estaba
para regar cada dedo
cada brote de alfalfa

fue la única vez que la vi sonreír
ese es el recuerdo más antiguo que tengo del amor

ALFALFA SPROUTS

My mother was made of bamboo
whenever the breeze moved her skirt
I saw the marks on her thin legs

my father would grab her willowy waist
and shake her like a stringless marionette

the last concubine
would do all the housework
if she didn't have a son

my mother's feet were a wheelbarrow
going going going
never tiring

I remember her sprawled on the grass
by the small pond
where the ducks always swam

with a porcelain jug I'd draw water
then go over to where she lay
and sprinkle every toe
every alfalfa sprout

that was the only time I saw her smile
it is my oldest memory of love

OTRO LIRIO

El anciano abre el cofre
y acaricia dos palomas dormidas

lo impulsa el deseo
unos pies tan pequeños

en el suelo las chinelas con peonías
muestran un ave que abanica su cola
y marca el territorio del cortejo

a lo lejos un reclamo
un grito timbrado

el flujo y el reflujo
las olas

la niña de vuelta al harén
con las mujeres solas

otra escoba de palacio
otra anciana que conspira
otro lirio

ANOTHER LILY

The old man opens the chest
and strokes two sleeping doves

he is driven by desire
such a dainty pair of feet

on the floor her slippers with peonies
show a bird that fans its tail
and marks the courtship territory

a plea from afar
a melodious call

the ebb and flow
of waves

the girl back to the harem
with the unmarried women

another palace broom
another conspiring old lady
another lily

AFUERA CROA UNA RANA

En la oscuridad
la sangre del emperador se inflama
ordena buscar a la nueva doncella

un temblor sacude el corazón de la niña
afuera croa una rana

han perfumado el agua con lilas
y en sus hombros reposan hojas de melocotón

el eunuco avanza con una linterna de papel encerado

detrás de las celosías sombras en movimiento
reflejan una lucha entre alces

entrelazan sus astas y forcejean
hasta que uno cede
y se entrega

ni siquiera con este deleite se conmueve
el emperador

después de desatar las cintas
brota la repugnancia por la belleza

OUTSIDE A FROG IS CROAKING

In the darkness
the emperor's blood sizzles
he sends for the new maiden

a tremor rattles the girl's heart
outside a frog is croaking

they have scented the water with lilacs
peach leaves adorn her shoulders

the eunuch approaches with a paper lantern

far from these jealousies moving shadows
reflect a battle between stags

they lock antlers and struggle
until one gives up
and surrenders

even this kind of pleasure does not move
the emperor

after untying the sashes
a revulsion for beauty takes root

EL LAGO DE LAS CINCO FLORES

En las cumbres cantan los fénix
y a mis pies bailan unicornios
toda la isla está poblada de faisanes
y dragones

vivo en un jardín
donde la primavera es eterna
y hay verdor en cipreses y pinos
melocotoneros en flor se doblan
cargados de frutos

aquí el agua es bendita

dos caballitos de mar
danzan ensartados bajo el agua
en un acuerdo atípico de maternidad
el hipocampo expulsa diminutos peces
y se regocija entre las hembras

sobre los altos bambúes
las ramas rozan las nubes donde el cielo se apoya

todo lo que el agua toca florecerá en árboles
frutos y flores

un árbol sembrado en el agua es un Buda
sonrisa iluminada
lleva allí cientos de años
y cada primavera florece para purificar
su ira en el espejo

FIVE FLOWER LAKE

Phoenixes sing from the peaks
and unicorns dance at my feet
the whole island is full of pheasants
and dragons

I live in a garden
where spring is eternal
cypresses and pines always green
peach trees in bloom bend over
laden with fruit

here the water is sacred

two seahorses
dance underwater intertwined
in an atypical parenting accord
the male ejects tiny fish
then revels among the females

above the high bamboo
branches brush the clouds that hold up the sky

everything the water touches will bloom on trees
fruits and flowers

a tree sown in water is a Buddha
enlightened smile
it's been there hundreds of years
and every spring it blooms to purify
its anger in the mirror

¿será el mismo árbol soñado cuando despierte?
o sólo un tronco podrido
testigo del ciclo de la vida

¿acaso el crimen no afecta la inmortalidad del árbol?

when I awake from my dream will the tree be the same
or just a rotted trunk
witness to the cycle of life?

does crime not affect the tree's immortality?

EL SALTO DEL TIGRE EN LA MALEZA

Mi padre era un carpintero
que deseaba un hijo varón
decía
la mujer el pasto
ha nacido para pisotearla

a los cuatro años
mi madre consultó a un adivino

una mujer fiel y sumisa
nace
si martillamos sus pies contra la madera
que no respiren ni se muevan
que sus dedos sean orugas

a los 15 años
había pasado por tres aldeas
ya sabía que el deseo
en los hombres viejos es una oportunidad

en un teatro local un joven acróbata
ensayaba la danza del cortejo
esa mañana mi abuelo fue a buscarme
te he comprado un esposo
un campesino honorable que trabaja la madera
complace a tu suegra
y ganarás el favor del cielo
entonces soñé con la emperatriz Leizu
genio de los gusanos de seda

A TIGER'S LEAP IN THE BRUSH

My father was a carpenter
who wanted a son
he'd say
women   grass
born to be stepped on

when I was four
my mother asked a soothsayer

a faithful, submissive woman
is born
if we nail her feet to the wood
so they can't move or breathe
so her toes become caterpillars

by 15
I had been through three towns
already knew that desire
in old men is an opportunity

at a local theater a young acrobat
rehearsed the courtship dance
that morning my grandfather came to find me
I have bought you a husband
an honorable peasant who works in wood
please your mother-in-law
and you'll gain heaven's favor
then I dreamed of Empress Leizu
the genius of silkworms

hay mujeres que nacen para ser pisoteadas
y otras para mandar entre aves de corral
pero tú no serás un pavo real entre gallinas
tu destino marcado está
por el salto del tigre en la maleza

a los 17 me casé con el señor Fei
mi abuelo ofreció una buena dote
pero rechacé la atadura de los pies

con tantas desavenencias
el señor Fei sacó su ábaco
sumó y restó
ningún beneficio con mis pies torcidos

toma tus cosas
vete
camina a otra aldea
busca el destino

a los 23 atravesé la llanura china
en busca del cuartel del dragón y el fénix
ahí me di cuenta de que perseguir el poder
es el salto del tigre en la maleza

no fue fácil vivir en una cueva
pero el dragón dijo
piedra tras piedra has derrumbado mis ciudades
¿te gustaría pisar cabezas?

some women are born to be stepped on
and others to reign among the barnyard fowl
but you will not be a peacock among hens
your fate is tied
to the tiger's leap in the brush

at 17 I married Mr. Fei
my grandfather offered a nice dowry
but I refused the foot-binding

with all these arguments
Mr. Fei took out his abacus
added and subtracted
no profit from my twisted feet

take your things
leave
go to another town
seek your fate

at 23 I crossed the plains of China
to seek the quarters of the dragon and phoenix
there I learned that the pursuit of power
is a tiger's leap in the brush

it wasn't easy living in a cave
but the dragon said
stone by stone you have torn down my cities
would you like to crush heads?

para lograr la obediencia
cubrí mi cabeza con un caparazón de tortuga
por treinta años

nunca olvidé las instrucciones del búho

no te muevas de la rama y dominarás el bosque
mira al gusano avanzar contráctil y en trozos
imita a los seres que fracturan su dolor
hasta alcanzar el salto del tigre en la maleza

to achieve obedience
I covered my head with a tortoise shell
for thirty years

never forgetting the owl's instructions

don't stray from the branch and you'll rule the forest
watch how the worm moves, contracting piece by piece
imitate the creatures that fracture their pain
until you can leap like a tiger in the brush

SALÓN DE LOS CRISANTEMOS

Deseaba esa voz para sí
que cantara en el Salón de los Crisantemos

una muchacha es un arroyo de montaña
que alborota el corazón con piedrecillas

un soldado necesita la belleza
en especial cuando el bosque ya no le habla
y a su paso todo calla

CHRYSANTHEMUM ROOM

He wanted that voice
to sing for him in the Chrysanthemum Room

a young woman is a mountain brook
whose tiny stones unsettle the heart

a soldier needs beauty
especially when the forest no longer speaks to him
and everything in his wake goes silent

LA CASA DE LAS BELLAS DURMIENTES

Cuando el cliente entra a la casa
pide los pies de la doncella dormida

al retiro de las chinelas
dos mariposas escapan por la ventana

el precio es alto
un ave fénix con plumas nuevas

afuera varios ancianos fuman opio
anhelan verla dormida

un manantial
es el sueño de la muchacha

al verla dormir
los dientes brotan
el cabello ennegrece

la inocente ignora
que la belleza
genera la unidad de las cosas

éxtasis

cuando despierta
retira el collar de naranja amarga
para bañarse
en el río que estalla en nueve fuentes

el té de la tarde invade el jardín

THE SLEEPING BEAUTY

When the client enters the house
he wants the feet of the sleeping maiden

as the slippers are lifted
two butterflies escape through the window

the price is high
a phoenix with new feathers

outside old men smoke opium
anxious to see her sleeping

a mountain spring
is the girl's dream

as they watch her sleep
their teeth sprout
their hair turns black

the innocent girl doesn't know
that beauty
spawns the unity of things

ecstasy

upon waking
she takes off the bitter orange necklace
to bathe
in the river of nine fountains

afternoon tea permeates the garden

PRESAGIO

Mi madre estaba sentada en el balcón

las manos engarzadas
estrujaban un clavel sobre el regazo
era su último verano con nosotros

un tremor invadió su cuerpo al sentir la llamada

la paloma agachada exhaló un soplido
un mal presagio

intenté tocarla y el ave saltó

un bajo murmullo salió de su pecho
hay que dejarla tranquila
no hace mal a nadie

pero tenía que sacarla

al sentir la amenaza eligió el vacío
el vuelo no llegó
sólo la catástrofe

en la calle no había rastro
una pluma cayó en remolino

algo de ella quedó adherido en mí
tiemblo si escucho el arrullo de una paloma

OMEN

My mother sat on the balcony

her entwined hands
clutching a carnation in her lap
it would be her last summer with us

a tremor invaded her body when she sensed the call

hunched the dove heaved a sigh
a bad omen

I tried to touch it but the bird jumped

from its breast came a faint murmur
just let it be
it won't hurt anyone

but I had to get rid of it

sensing a threat it chose the void
flight didn't come
only catastrophe

no trace left on the street
a feather spiraled downward

some of the bird remained within me
hearing a dove coo makes me shudder

sólo hasta que mueve su pico
y se apresta a iniciar el cortejo
respiro aliviada y la bendigo

only when it moves its beak
and begins the rites of courtship
can I breathe again and give my blessing

MY ENTERTAINMENT

En esa forzada holganza
miraba gusanos de seda

no requerían del bosque
ni necesitaban luz

era amable la oruga
en su cajón de madera

confraternizaba
y devoraba hojas

era un espectáculo verlos amarse
engarzar sus cuerpos en esa batalla fingida

para ver las pasiones basta un insecto

se atacan
se comen
se destrozan

copular es sagrado para el insecto
siempre sobrevive la especie

eran mi circo privado
my entertainment

MY ENTERTAINMENT

In that imposed leisure
I watched the silk worms

they didn't need the forest
didn't require light

the caterpillar was gentle
in its wooden box

it fraternized
and devoured leaves

quite a show it was to see them mate
entangle their bodies in fake battle

to witness passion an insect is enough

they attack each other
eat each other
tear each other to pieces

copulation is sacred to the insect
the species always survives

they were my private circus
my entertainment

GUARDIAS ROJOS

En esa ciudad antigua
las doncellas eran ofrendas
y la esposa vieja
discreta

cada noche una virgen nutría a mi amado

de la boca desdentada colgaban filos
lo ácido del beso

eran los años de la sífilis

después llegó el tremor
y sin alas sus manos aleteaban

cayeron sus dientes
pero nunca fue manso

vi a las doncellas cruzar el puente
hacia la cámara roja
y a los peces en el estanque
hibernar en el hielo

un oprobio que acepté
mientras adiestraba a los cuervos

un pequeño entrenamiento de maldad
que purificó mi corazón

RED GUARDS

In that ancient city
the maidens were gifts
and the old wife
discreet

each night a virgin nourished my beloved

barbs hung from his toothless mouth
the bitterness of kisses

it was the time of syphilis

then the tremors arrived
his wingless hands fluttered

his teeth fell out
but he was never tame

I saw the maidens crossing the bridge
on their way to the red chamber
and the fish in the pond
hibernating in ice

a disgrace to bear
while I trained the crows

a minor exercise in evil
that cleansed my heart

MIL GRULLAS

Conozco el entorno del bosque
ese abalanzarse contra el cielo en alada sincronía

el grito de un ave de tormenta precipita el regreso a los nidos
y los débiles caen sin que el enjambre lo note

desde aquí veo pasar a tres niños
con ofrendas a sus antepasados

los esperé toda la tarde
pero sólo vi bajar el arroyo de lava

una grulla bebe agua en el patio antes de seguir a la bandada
lo sentí un buen augurio

ya vienen los guardias por mi
sin costureras ni asistentes de baño

antes de partir enjuago los malos espíritus
que anidan en mis ropas

ahora que en mis bosques hay vida
y fuentes en mis orificios
en mi corazón aletea un colibrí

A THOUSAND CRANES

I know the forest world
how they rush toward the sky in winged synchrony

a storm bird's cry hastens a return to the nests
the weak ones fall unnoticed by the swarm

from here I see three children pass by
with offerings for their ancestors

I waited for them all afternoon
but saw only the stream of lava come down

one crane drinks water in the courtyard before joining the flock
I took it as a good omen

already the guards are coming for me
without seamstress or bath attendant

before leaving I rinse the evil spirits
that have nested in my garments

now that there is life in my forests
and fountains in every orifice
a hummingbird flutters in my heart

EL SEGUNDO ESPOSO

Teníamos por costumbre
andar por el bosque de abedules
y repasar con los dedos la madera
hasta sentir la estela de ceniza
que dejaba la navaja en la corteza

los dioses
me tendieron una trampa

¿qué otra explicación para mi gran error?

cuando Yu Qiwei se ocultó en el bosque
viví con Chao
quien me aseguraba su muerte

pero cuando Yu Qiwei regresó
fui repudiada
a pesar de que él sabía
que tomaría un tren a Beijing esa tarde

ha sido mi única vergüenza

años después regresé a esos árboles
a esos abedules blancos
y encontré que a pesar de la intemperie
nuestros nombres seguían en la corteza

entonces tomé el valor de un abedul
y dejé que la navaja
tatuara en mi espalda una estrella

THE SECOND HUSBAND

We had a ritual
of strolling through the birch forest
grazing the wood with our fingers
until we felt the trail of ashes
that the blade left on the bark

the gods
set a trap for me

how else to explain my great mistake?

when Yu Qiwei fled into the forest
I lived with Chao
who assured me he was dead

but when Yu Qiwei returned
I was rejected
though he knew
he'd be on a train to Beijing that night

that was my only disgrace

years later I returned to those trees
those white birches
and despite the elements
our names remained on the bark

so drawing courage from a birch
I let the blade
tattoo a star on my back

en noches de luna
ese rayo de luz
deja ver a la muchacha que era
y me ayuda a sobrellevar el día

on moonlit nights
that ray of light
reveals the young woman I once was
and helps me get through the day

ALAS PLUMOSAS

De los huevos nacían larvas
y de las orugas crisálidas

libres de prejuicios
erguían árboles

penetraban los orificios más húmedos

en ese universo portátil
ninfas desnudas

un reality show

eran tan exhibicionistas
que copulaban delante de los niños

se habían domesticado en cautividad

otros gusanos se alimentaban de cadáveres
pero los míos masticaban con fruición
hojas de morera

para espiarlos sólo necesitaba una lámpara
y una pequeña lupa

tanto tiempo perdido con las hojas
para que la mariposa de alas plumosas
jamás aprendiera a volar

FEATHER-WINGED

From the eggs larvae were born
and from the caterpillars, chrysalises

free of prejudice
they erected trees

and penetrated the dampest openings

in that portable universe
naked nymphs

a reality show

such exhibitionists
they even copulated in front of the children

in captivity they had been domesticated

other worms fed on cadavers
but mine relished in chewing
mulberry leaves

to spy them all I needed was a lamp
and a small magnifying glass

so much time wasted in the leaves
but the feather-winged moth
never would learn to fly

EL GATO DE LA EMPERATRIZ WU

Durante el exilio en el Jardín de la Quietud
aprendí a contener la violencia
como el gato de la emperatriz Wu

una mañana mientras meditaba cerca del lago
me visitó un dios
vestido de seda y de apariencia de mono

no sé si fueron tantos mimos
pero con el tiempo se volvió carnívoro
y los criados le temían

cuando llegaban los espías
lo saludaban con una venia
en prueba de rectitud política

me gustaba verlos correr por el jardín de orquídeas
cuando él pasaba volando sobre sus cabezas

al terminar mi exilio
regresé a la Ciudad Prohibida

quise que mi mono imitara al gato de la emperatriz Wu
que contuvo sus instintos
y convivió en una jaula con impasibles loros

pero era salvaje
y mordía

un amigo leal
al que tuve que sacrificar

EMPRESS WU'S CAT

During my exile in the Garden of Stillness
I learned to suppress violence
like Empress Wu's cat

one morning as I meditated by the lake
a god visited me
in silk robes and the guise of a monkey

maybe from too much cuddling
over time he became carnivorous
and the servants feared him

whenever the spies came
they bowed before him
to prove their political correctness

I liked watching them run through the orchids
when he came flying over their heads

after the exile
I returned to the Forbidden City

if only my monkey had suppressed its instincts
like Empress Wu's cat
who shared a cage with indifferent parrots

but he was wild
and would bite

a loyal friend
whom I had to sacrifice

COLORES DE LA VIOLENCIA

El día de limpieza de las tumbas
dejaban poemas en las gradas
de Tiananmen Square

aún se atrevían
a escribir contra mí

en el Gran salón del Pueblo
saqué pinceles de colores
y coloqué sobre la mesa vasijas para el agua

nada como la sangre para colorear las azaleas

en los jarrones
las flores de ciruelo
caían sobre los crisantemos
para confundir las estaciones del año

quería pintar un pájaro amarillo
que en la ventana picoteaba una naranja
pero al tomar firme el pincel
del papel se desprendió un carruaje tirado por caballos
y cayó en desbandada por el precipicio

mi mano suspendida en el aire
no logró frenar este amasijo de patas
ni impidió que los colores de la violencia
cubrieran de sangre Tiananmen Square

COLORS OF VIOLENCE

On Tomb Sweeping Day
they left poems on the steps
of Tiananmen Square

they still dared
to write against me

in the Great Hall of the People
I took out paintbrushes
placed bowls for water on the table

nothing like blood for painting azaleas

in the vases
plum blossoms
scattered over the chrysanthemums
to confuse the seasons

I wanted to paint a yellow bird
pecking at an orange in the window
but when I grasped the brush
from the paper emerged a carriage pulled by horses
that fell off the cliff head over heels

my hand suspended in the air
could not stop that jumble of hooves
nor prevent the colors of violence
spreading blood over Tiananmen Square

LLUVIA

Esa noche celebramos el Festival de la Luna
una botella de vino imperial
servido en vasos de la dinastía Ming

volví a preguntar a mi esposo
¿dónde está mi ejército?

trabajando la tierra
deben proteger a los campesinos
de las tentaciones del feudalismo

pero era la estación lluviosa
y los tractores en el fango
eran ranas con las piernas cortadas

RAIN

That night we celebrated the Moon Festival
a bottle of imperial wine
served in Ming Dynasty crystal

I asked my husband again
where is my army?

working the land
they must protect the peasants
from the temptations of feudalism

but it was the rainy season
and in the mud the tractors
were frogs with severed legs

CRÍA CUERVOS

Me he quedado
a merced de la turba

dónde está mi guardia
esos hermosos jóvenes
con ojos de pez

comían mendrugos de mi mano
ahora me desconocen

detrás del filo cortante
que acaricia mi garganta

el zumbido del enjambre

IF YOU RAISE CROWS

I am left
at the mercy of the mob

where are my guards
those handsome young men
with their fish eyes

they used to eat from my hand
now they deny knowing me

beyond the sharp blade
caressing my throat

the buzz of the swarm

VOLVER AL CAMPO

Las mujeres molían granos
para un cocido de verduras

inminente era la noche
y debían trabajar rápido porque las lámparas
estaban prohibidas

cuando sonó el gong que anuncia la comida
los soldados no compartieron el alimento
con los campesinos

a la mañana siguiente la mitad de ellos
había denunciado a sus padres
y la otra llevaba carteles en sus cuerpos
condenados a una muerte segura

la orden era subir a la montaña
vivir entre lo elevado y lo pequeño
pero el cielo respondió con inundaciones

entonces regresaron a las ciudades
en busca de carroña

ése era mi ejército
cuervos hambrientos

RETURN TO THE COUNTRYSIDE

Women pounded the grain
for a vegetable stew

night was imminent
they had to hurry because lanterns
were forbidden

when the gong called for dinner
the soldiers did not share the meal
with the peasants

the next morning half of them
had denounced their parents
the other half wore posters on their bodies
condemned to certain death

the order was to climb the mountain
to live up in the heights among the lowliest
but the sky answered with floods

so they returned to the cities
looking for carrion

that was my army
ravenous crows

MANCHURIA – SHANGHAI – PEKÍN

Cuando un dios disfruta
no piensa en salvar a nadie

de nada sirvió reclamar mis derechos de esposa
en mí latía el corazón de una criada

mientras los indigentes se apuñaleaban entre sí
yo revisaba los mapas
Shanghai y Pekín caerían primero
Manchuria ya estaba rendida

cada pelea comenzaba con una venia
y terminaba en un crimen

llevaba mi sol sobre la espalda
y en algún lugar lo perdí

MANCHURIA – SHANGHAI – PEKING

When a god is enjoying life
he doesn't think to save anyone

claiming my rights as wife made no difference
the heart of a servant thrummed within me

while the beggars stabbed each other
I went over the maps
Shanghai and Peking would fall first
Manchuria had already surrendered

every fight began with a bow
and ended in a crime

I had carried the sun on my back
but somewhere I lost hold

EN UNA VASIJA

En una vasija guardo incienso humano
para los dioses
así como el rocío necesita la rosa
la maldad es necesaria para gobernar un reino

IN A VESSEL

In a vessel I keep human incense
for the gods
just as the dew needs the rose
evil is essential to govern a kingdom

DE UNA LEYENDA CHINA

Para satisfacer a sus generales
el emperador Tang Li
ordenó ahorcar a su amante
la dama Yang

ella sabía que a pesar de disfrutar
de los favores de la corte
una soga estaba en su destino

ser la favorita
no hacía más que recordarle
la caída de las flores del ciruelo
al final del invierno

después de su muerte
cada año un paisaje nevado
traía de vuelta a la dama Yang

así fue como los obligó
a venerarla en invierno

FROM A CHINESE LEGEND

To satisfy his generals
Emperor Tang Li
ordered the hanging of his mistress
Lady Yang

she knew that despite enjoying
the favor of the court
a noose was in her future

being the favorite
only served to remind her
of plum blossoms falling
at winter's end

after her death
each year a snowy landscape
would bring Lady Yang back

this is how he forced them
to worship her in winter

DEMONIO DE HUESOS BLANCOS

Soy Jiang Qing
la cuarta esposa
me llamaban demonio de huesos blancos
cuando él me besaba
sentía la lengua de la bestia
anidando en mi cuerpo

mi fidelidad me acreditaba como hiena
si él me decía ataca
yo atacaba
el ejército era mi daga
yo era el perro de mi amo
su hueso
su lado oscuro

sería clavada adentro de su ataúd
esas eran sus palabras

embalsamado parecía un bagre

alguien escribía palabras obscenas
sobre mi piel

venía acompañado por dos músicos
provenientes de la misma tumba

yo enhebraba una aguja
y cosía mis ojos para no verlo

lloraba el laúd monótonos rezos

WHITE-BONED DEMON

I am Jiang Qing
the fourth wife
they called me the white-boned demon
when he kissed me
I felt the tongue of the beast
nesting in my body

my loyalty proved me a hyena
if he said attack
I attacked
the army was my dagger
I was my master's dog
his bone
his dark side

I would be nailed inside his coffin
those were his words

embalmed he looked like a catfish

someone was writing obscenities
on my skin

he was accompanied by two musicians
coming from the same grave

I kept threading a needle and sewing my eyes shut
so I wouldn't see him

the lute cried monotonous prayers

era la viuda
la tarántula

quienes conocían mi jardín
se escondían debajo de las piedras

I was the widow
the tarantula

everyone who knew my garden
hid beneath the stones

EL DIFUNTO

Una noche de relámpagos
el difunto regresó

con los ojos cubiertos
de placas de jade

rompió objetos
hizo ruido

la brisa movía el árbol de monedas
para traer abundancia

sobre la piedra disolvió tinta negra
y escribió dos líneas

he perdido mi álamo erguido
y tú perdiste tu sauce

versos de un poema para su segunda esposa
la joven asesinada en Changsha

tarde aprendí el peligro de un amor desmedido

THE DEAD MAN

One night when lightning struck
the dead man came back

his eyes covered
by jade plates

he broke things
made a racket

the breeze swayed the coin tree
to usher in abundance

on the stone he mixed black ink
and wrote two lines

I lost my proud poplar
and you your willow

verses from a poem for his second wife
the young woman killed in Changsha

I learned late the danger of loving too much

SÓLO OBEDECÍA ÓRDENES

Una mantis extiende sus patas y presiona la presa

hay atenuantes
sólo obedecía órdenes

junto al incensario
un resto de piel de conejo
hace a la madera despedir fragancia

cómo puedo calentar el hogar
si todas las grullas pasan hacia el norte
sin detenerse a beber agua

JUST FOLLOWING ORDERS

With its forelegs a mantis pins down its prey

there are circumstances
just following orders

a strip of rabbit fur
by the incense burner
triggers the wood's fragrance

how can I warm the hearth
when all the cranes fly over to the north
without stopping to drink water

BONSAI

Que el hombre no ame nada
y será invulnerable
—Chuang Tzé

Cuando veo pasar las nubes pienso en dragones
mi alrededor es blanco
inhalo opio y traspaso la luna
plácido es flotar en el sueño
sobre dragones de humo

afianzado sobre una bandeja
el pequeño árbol desconoce el tiempo
el alambre tuerce sus ramas
y lo obliga a ser el viento

sus cortas raíces no alcanzan la muerte
a pesar de que es la hora del olvido

tantos crímenes
tantas venganzas

con indiferencia dice
hasta cuándo la luz acariciará las ramas

BONSAI

Let man love nothing
and he will be invulnerable
—Chuang Tzé

When I see passing clouds I think of dragons
white surrounds me
I inhale opium and seep through the moon
how peaceful to float in dreams
over dragons of smoke

holding firm to a tray
the tiny tree knows nothing of time
wire twists its branches
forcing it to become wind

though the time for oblivion has arrived
its short roots cannot reach death

so many crimes
so much revenge

with indifference it says
how much longer will the light stroke my branches

PARA SER EMPERATRIZ

Para ser emperatriz
no bastaba
el sello de jade
ni entrelazar las escamas
en el lecho imperial
necesitaba una armadura de piedra
un corazón de lagarto
y engullir entero

pero cuanto más alto es el árbol
más larga es su sombra

cuando se vive tan cerca del peligro
debemos arreglar la tumba
con pieles de osos
soldados de terracota
y amuletos de jade

cuando se vive tan cerca del peligro
debemos conocer el camino
a la Vía de los Espíritus
y esperar la bondad de los dioses

cuando se vive tan cerca del peligro
la sombra del árbol
no debe arroparnos

TO BE EMPRESS

To be empress
it wasn't enough
to have a jade seal
or to ravel our scales
on the imperial bed
I needed an armor of rock
the heart of a lizard
and to swallow things whole

but the taller the tree
the longer its shadow

when you live so close to danger
you must prepare your grave
with bear skins
clay soldiers
jade amulets

when you live so close to danger
you must learn the way
to the Spirit Path
and hope for mercy from the gods

when you live so close to danger
you must not take shelter
in the shadow of the tree

EL AIRE DE SIBERIA

Mi lengua es un gong oxidado
que no artícula palabras
sólo hablo con las rosas dibujadas
en el biombo que separa una cama de la otra
pero el reflejo de la rosa no es la rosa
la verdadera rosa se desnuda

pétalo a pétalo cae la pureza
rosa marchita
entre las brasas

en este lugar es difícil resistir la noche
y en la espera me pregunto
¿qué es esa llama que me abrasa?
la respuesta es el silencio
un dardo inmóvil en mi corazón

sé que la muerte viene por la garganta
una soga de pañuelos
debe ser tan fuerte como una mentira

¿qué es lo que quieren que confiese?

una sala con ocho camas verdes
aquí me dejaron
en este espacio sin retorno
debo acostumbrarme a prescindir de las cosas

sólo el ciruelo sabe cuánto duele el invierno

THE CHILL OF SIBERIA

My tongue is a rusted gong
that utters no words
I speak only to the roses etched
on the screen that divides bed from bed
but the reflection of a rose is not a rose
a real rose sheds its layers

petal by petal purity falls
a wilted rose
among the embers

here the night is hard to endure
waiting I ask myself
what is this flame that sears me?
the response is silence
a tiny spear lodged in my heart

I know death enters by the throat
a rope made of handkerchiefs
must be as strong as a lie

what do they want me to confess?

a room with eight green beds
they left me here
in this space of no return
I must learn to do without

only the plum tree knows how winter hurts

HOSPITAL DE MOSCÚ

En lo subterráneo
las deudas se pagan día a día

bajo las lámparas de neón
la dura camilla
una expiación

viviría con los zorros
y las lechuzas

a pesar del pronóstico
volví fuerte
una secuoya gigante
que rozaba las nubes

HOSPITAL IN MOSCOW

Underground
debts are repaid day after day

beneath the neon lamps
the stiff bed
a kind of expiation

I would dwell with the foxes
and the owls

despite the prognosis
I came back strong
a giant sequoia
brushing against the clouds

PRIMAVERA

Para saludarte mañana
nada mejor que un pájaro
cantando en la ventana
plumaje de huesos ven
insemina el día

SPRING

To greet you morning
what better than a bird
singing at the window
plumage of bones come
inseminate the day

MI TERCER ESPOSO

Llevo un letrero entre el pecho y la espalda
rata
me gritan los niños

hoy el jurado traerá de testigo
a mi tercer esposo
un cuarto caliente en invierno

la tarde en que me casé con Tang Na
llevaba un vestido rojo y una orquídea en el pecho
de eso queda una foto en la Pagoda

Tang Na era débil
bebió cien cabezas de fósforos
la noche en que abandoné Shanghai

nada pude contra esta sombra
que escupe su verdad podrida

soy un ciervo que espera al cazador
en medio del campo
aunque presiento la bala
no puedo saltar

MY THIRD HUSBAND

Inside me I bear a label
rat
scream the children

today the jury will bring in as witness
my third husband
a warm room in winter

that afternoon when I married Tang Na
I wore a red dress and an orchid on my chest
all that's left is a photo at the Pagoda

Tang Na was weak
he swallowed a hundred match heads
the night I left Shanghai

I could do nothing against this shadow
that spits its rotted truth

I am a deer awaiting the hunter
in an open field
though I sense a bullet coming
I cannot leap

ENSÉÑAME ÁRBOL

Un rayo de luz cae sobre mi caja
en ella suceden cosas
en ella reposa el circo de mi amo

sólo aspiro al perdón del árbol
que el ruiseñor esté pendiente de las hojas

el crimen no afecta al árbol
está cautivo en mis ojos
en las ramas y en sus frutos

cuando pasen las grullas comenzaré la poda
y en primavera vendrán nuevos brotes

ahora exhibe ese aspecto de madera muerta
que da la impresión de que fuese muy viejo

enséñame árbol
la quietud
para atraer a los pájaros

TEACH ME TREE

A ray of light shines on my box
there things happen
there lies my master's circus

all I want is the tree's forgiveness
let the nightingale tend its leaves

crime has no effect on the tree
it is trapped in my eyes
in its branches and fruits

when the cranes fly over I will start to prune
and new buds will come up in spring

but now it has the look of dead wood
the illusion of being very old

teach me tree
the stillness
that lures the birds

TEMPLO

Esta mañana vinieron los guardias
no tocaron mi caja de gusanos
ni lograron mover el árbol

no saben que son mis parientes

en este túmulo verde
los insectos son solidarios con la desgracia
en mis cejas hay ciudades
y en mis orejas reinos

ahora que me sedimento
soy un templo para la naturaleza

TEMPLE

This morning the guards came
didn't touch my box of worms
couldn't move the tree

they don't know these are my kin

on this green burial mound
the insects side with misfortune
there are cities on my brow
kingdoms in my ears

now as I become sediment
I am nature's temple

CONTRA LA NADA

Acostúmbrate cuerpo
al blanco ceroso de los techos
donde bandadas de pájaros se estrellan
contra la nada

acostúmbrate cuerpo a este catre
donde reposan conmigo chinches y pulgas

ahora que sientes la fatiga de la culpa
no tirites
no hay frío

somete al olvido tu voluntad

aprende a escuchar el grillo
y su canción de todo el año

acostúmbrate cuerpo a la indiferencia
con que la noche sacrifica el día

la ingratitud de la plebe
es un cristal opaco

ahora que la venganza es un boomerang
desean que ataje el hueso del amo

¿por qué tengo que pagar por esas muertes?

no soy mujer que asusten esas lápidas vacías

INTO THE VOID

Body get used to this
ceilings white as wax
where flocks of birds crash
into the void

body get used to this cot
where bedbugs and fleas nestle with me

now that guilt weighs on you
do not shiver
it is not cold

surrender your will to oblivion

learn to listen to the cricket
and its never-ending song

body get used to the indifference
of night as it sacrifices day

the ingratitude of the masses
is opaque glass

now that vengeance is a boomerang
they want me to catch the master's bone

why should I pay for those deaths?

I'm not a woman scared by those empty tombs

EL ABRIGO DE ASTRACÁN

Caminaba al matadero
ignoraba
que para un abrigo
había que desollar treinta fetos

en estos años de encierro
fue cubierto mi cuerpo
por piel no nacida

esperaba la sentencia
sobre un cuchillo afilado

cada noche
cercenaba un cordero

pero el cuchillo era indócil
y el descarnado
huía sin dejar el codiciado rizo

THE ASTRAKHAN COAT

Walking to the slaughterhouse
I didn't know
that to make a coat
thirty fetuses must be flayed

closed in all these years
my body was covered
by unborn fur

I awaited my sentence
on the sharp edge of a knife

every night
I'd dismember a lamb

but the knife was unruly
and the naked animal
would escape with its coveted curl

LA CAJA

La escarcha cubre el paisaje donde pocas aves trinan
otro invierno en cautiverio

bajo la luna un ave intenta un nido

la pared filtra un graznido
notas puras
sin armónicos

en la caja
el gorjeo del harén es intenso

animados por cantos de apareamiento
los gusanos segregan cera

¿cómo abrigar un cuerpo húmedo?

una lámpara de aceite es todo lo que tengo
y no produce calor suficiente para las crías

algunos se devoran entre sí
porque en el peligro no existe la piedad

THE BOX

Frost covers the landscape where few birds sing
another winter in captivity

in moonlight a bird attempts a nest

a squawk seeps through the wall
pure notes
without harmonics

in the box
the harem's chirping is intense

animated by mating calls
the worms secrete wax

how to warm a damp body?

an oil lamp is all I have
not enough heat for the young

some feast on each other
when danger looms there is no mercy

HÁBLAME ÁRBOL

Las alas blancas de las grullas
sobre el azul del cielo

hoy cumplo 77 años
debo hablar ante el jurado
es difícil explicar por qué arrastro mi fama
en este carro de estiércol

¿cuándo dejó de importarme
si el verdugo mata
o el vencido implora?

al salir de esta celda
un alacrán me prestará su veneno

afuera están cosechando deudas

dicen que cavé tantas tumbas
que no hay cuerpos suficientes para llenarlas

anoche un cuervo no paró de chillar
y hoy el árbol amaneció sin hojas

si un solo sentimiento conociera el árbol
caería fulminado a mis pies

háblame árbol
qué sientes encriptado en la madera
sólo el viento se atreve con tus hojas

SPEAK TO ME TREE

The cranes' white wings
against the blue of sky

today my 77th birthday
I must speak before the jury
hard to explain why I must drag my fame
on this cart of manure

when did I stop caring
whether the executioner kills
or the vanquished pleads?

when I leave this cell
a scorpion will lend me its poison

outside they are collecting debts

they say I dug so many graves
there are not enough corpses to fill them

last night a crow would not stop cawing
and by dawn the tree had shed its leaves

if the tree could feel just one emotion
it would fall stricken at my feet

speak to me tree
what feeling lives encrypted in your wood
only the wind dares touch your leaves

eres menos viejo que el río
pero tu paciencia supera a la montaña

enséñame esa manera tuya de recibir el rayo
a mantener inclinada mi cabeza
cuando el fuego alcance mis huesos

you are not as old as the river
but your patience surpasses the mountain

teach me your secret way to absorb lightning
how to keep my head bowed
when the fire reaches my bones

CONFESIÓN DE LA MADRE DE LA MUCHACHA

Ella era una ramita
que recibía el favor de los dioses

llevaba el sol en la espalda

le advertía
que no había enemigo pequeño
y que un mosquito puede matar a un hombre

pero ella gozaba
con los huesos

agachada sobre un campo de arroz
me llega el aroma fétido de la ciénaga
y tiemblo

no es mucho lo que puedo decir

la última vez que la vi tenía cinco años
y dormía

esta noche
cuando la luna se derrame sobre el patio
el halcón vendrá por mí

me humillo ante mis dioses
y ruego por un tránsito perfecto
al mundo de mis antepasados

debo lavar mis ropas y cruzar el Río Amarillo

THE GIRL'S MOTHER CONFESSES

She was a tender branch
who won the gods' favor

she carried the sun on her back

I warned her
that no enemy was small
that a mosquito could kill a man

but she found pleasure
in bones

bent over in a rice field
the stench of swamp reaches me
and I tremble

there's not much I can say

last time I saw her she was only five
and asleep

tonight
when the moon spills over the yard
the falcon will come for me

I humble myself before my gods
and plead for a perfect transit
to the world of my ancestors

I must wash my clothes and cross the Yellow River

en algún lugar de esos caminos
esperaré a mi muchacha

siento pena
porque cuando la dejé dormida
el sol caía sobre su espalda

somewhere along those roads
I'll wait for my child

how I regret
leaving while she slept
with the sun falling on her back

DE CÓMO LOGRÉ SER ESPOSA

Un ejército de cangrejos rojos
atraviesan el patio

los hombres comen la carne blanca

el dragón levanta la mirada
una joven uniformada no es un soldado

ella sabe que él viaja
pisando cadáveres

bailan sobre la hierba
hasta que cesa la danza del grillo

tiembla
pero su madre le enseñó
a no tener hígado de lirio

gacela
una litera de crisantemos
te aguarda

ON HOW I BECAME A WIFE

An army of red crabs
traverses the patio

the men eat the white meat

the dragon lifts his gaze
a girl in uniform is not a soldier

she knows how he travels
trampling corpses

they dance on the grass
until the cricket song dies out

she trembles
but her mother taught her
not to be faint of heart

gazelle
a berth of chrysanthemums
awaits you

UN NIDO

Un capullo con la crisálida dentro
ha caído en mi taza de té

un milagro de la emperatriz Leizu
anuncia una oruga en primavera

la lluvia me sorprende con ese ovillo en mi mano

no romperé el hilo
hasta que ella transforme el alimento en seda
para entonces la avaricia juntará muchas hojas

caja nido son mis manos
cóncavo cáliz

laborioso capullo teje el ovillo en oro

¿sobrevivirá con mi tibio aliento?

A NEST

A cocoon with chrysalis inside
has landed in my teacup

a miracle of the Empress Leizu
heralds a caterpillar in spring

rain finds me holding this clew in my hand

I will not break the thread
until it transforms food into silk
by then greed will have gathered many leaves

box nest my two hands
an open chalice

industrious cocoon weaves the clew into gold

will it survive with just my warm breath?

LA VISITA DE MI HIJA NA

Hubo un tiempo en que amé más allá del dolor
un tiempo en el cual de cada hombre deseaba un hijo

de niña cazaba conejos
los asaba en un fuego rústico
después limpiaba sus huesos y los hacía collares

de esa niña sólo queda un ligero impulso
por armar trampas

ayúdame hija
sálvame de una bala en la cabeza

¿por qué te avergüenzas de mí?
una viuda es un ave con un ala

cuando vengas a despedirte trae papel celofán
y envuelve mi corazón que aún palpita

MY DAUGHTER NA'S VISIT

There was a time when I loved deeper than I suffered
a time when from every man I desired a child

as a girl I'd hunt rabbits
roast them on a crude fire
then clean their bones and string necklaces

nothing's left of that girl but a faint penchant
for setting traps

daughter help me
save me from a bullet to the head

why are you ashamed of me?
a widow is a bird with just one wing

when you come to say goodbye bring cellophane
to wrap my heart tender and throbbing

CRISÁLIDA

Al perder la facultad del vuelo
optan por reproducirse con esmero

a través de los pelos olfatorios
perciben los aromas
protuberancias carnosas
chupan y chupan feromonas de las hembras

un condenado
puede hablar con los muertos

había que acabar con los cuatro viejos
el pensamiento antiguo
las costumbres
la cultura tradicional
la historia

destruir para construir

soy la montaña
que sigue ahí cuando despierto

horas de copulación
tejen el dorado hilo
que sujeta la mariposa al vuelo

yo también fui crisálida

CHRYSALIS

When they lose the ability to fly
they opt to reproduce in earnest

through their olfactory hairs
they sense the aromas
fleshy protuberances
suck and suck the females' pheromones

the condemned
can talk with the dead

we had to get rid of the four old men
ancient thinking
customs
traditional culture
history

destroy in order to build

I am the mountain
that's still there when I wake

hours of copulation
weave the golden thread
that holds the moth in flight

I too was a chrysalis

OBEDIENCIA

La pareja de ocas vuela hacia el norte
graznidos de amor hieren mi corazón
a pesar de mi insistencia
ningún mensaje cayó del cielo

el sol trae bandadas de pájaros

el equilibrio está en la unión
la fuerza en la falange
que obedece al líder

después de atravesar las nubes
¿quién no regresaría contento al nido?

OBEDIENCE

A pair of geese fly north
their love calls wound my heart
despite my persistence
no message came down from heaven

the sun brings flocks of birds

balance is found in unity
strength in the phalanx
that obeys the leader

after traversing the clouds
who wouldn't gladly return to the nest?

TESTAMENTO ARBÓREO

Ninguna araña drenará veneno
ni pájaro carpintero horadará la madera
sólo la alondra que canta en vuelo
podrá pisar sus altas ramas

fue la raíz quien firmó el pacto

TREE TESTAMENT

No spider shall drain poison
nor woodpecker bore through the bark
only the lark that sings in flight
may alight on its highest branches

it was the root that signed the pact

QUE ME VEA UNA ALONDRA

Sé que las leyes de Newton producen cantos
de allí la tenacidad de la alondra
la forma como sostiene su canto en el aire
conteniendo y soltando su voz de arroyo

el comedero colgante está provisto de fruta
y la jaula engastada en oro
pero no entiendo el impedimento del pájaro

afuera el alpiste de hielo

otras aves se acercan a picotear la fruta
ella se estrella en la nieve

ramita a ramita construye un nido

aunque imite el cantar de la alondra
soy una mujer cautiva

para modular
necesito el vibrato de otra garganta

me hallo en el trono de la muerte

necesito que me vea una alondra
que la muerte pierda su dominio
porque una alondra puede revocar la sentencia
si un moribundo encuentra sus ojos

LARK PLEASE LOOK AT ME

I know Newton's laws produce birdsongs
hence the tenacity of the lark
how it carries its song through the air
holding and releasing its river voice

the hanging feeder is replete with fruit
and the cage set in gold
I can't understand what impedes her

outside the birdseed now ice

other birds come to peck the fruit
she crashes into the snow

twig by twig she builds a nest

though I try to sing like the lark
I am a woman imprisoned

unable to modulate
without the vibrato of another throat

I find myself at the throne of death

lark please look at me
and death shall have no dominion
because a lark can revoke the sentence
if a dying person meets its eye

NOTES

"*The Sleeping Beauty*": The title comes from a Japanese novel, translated into English as *The Sleeping Beauty* and into Spanish as *La casa de las bellas durmientes.*

"The Dead Man": The italicized lines are the first verse of a poem by Mao Zedong, rendered in English by Willis Barnstone as "The Gods" (in *The Poems of Mao Zedong*, Berkeley: University of California, 1972, p. 87):

> I lost my proud poplar and you your willow
> As poplar and willow they soar straight up
> into the ninth heaven
> and ask the prisoner of the moon, Wu Gang, what is there.
> He offers them wine from the cassia tree.
>
> The lonely lady on the moon, Chang E,
> spreads her vast sleeves
> and dances for these good souls in the unending sky.
> Down on earth a sudden report of the tiger's defeat.
> Tears fly down from a great upturned bowl of rain.

CHRONOLOGY: JIANG QING, MAO ZEDONG, AND TWENTIETH-CENTURY CHINA

1914: Jiang (originally named Li Yunhe) is born in Zhucheng, Shandong Province, on March 19, to a concubine who is mistreated by her husband.

1920s: Jiang and her mother move to Jinan to live with her grandparents.

1928: Jiang's mother dies, leaving her an orphan at age fourteen. She runs away from her grandparents to join a theater troupe.

1930: Jiang's first marriage to an older businessman, Pei Minglun, lasts only a few months; at age sixteen, she leaves her family to go to Beijing with a traveling theater company.

Early 1930s: Jiang moves to Qingdao, where she meets and marries Yu Qiwei, a student revolutionary. She joins the Chinese Communist Party (CCP) and is briefly arrested for Communist activities.

1935: Jiang moves to Shanghai and joins a theater company; with the stage name Lan Ping, she becomes a famous actress.

1936: Jiang marries art critic Tang Na. After a tumultuous relationship, the couple separate in 1937.

1937: Beginning of Sino-Japanese War and invasion of Shanghai. Jiang leaves Shanghai for Yan'an, the base of the CCP, of which Mao Zedong is the leader.

1938–39: Jiang meets and marries Mao Zedong; Party leaders are against the marriage, but finally agree on the condition that Jiang stay out of politics for twenty years.

1940: Birth of Jiang's only child, daughter Li Na.

1940s: Mao continues to lead the CCP in Yan'an; Jiang serves as his secretary.

1945: End of Sino-Japanese War and World War II when the U.S. drops atomic bombs on Hiroshima and Nagasaki.

1946–49: Chinese Civil War between the Communists and the ruling Nationalists; Communist victory establishes Mao as leader of the People's Republic of China in 1949.

1950s: Jiang suffers from poor health; spends time in Moscow for treatment.

1966: Jiang becomes key figure in the Cultural Revolution as a leader of the politically powerful Gang of Four.

1970s: Although Jiang continues to wield power, she and Mao live apart.

1976: Death of Mao Zedong, September 9. Jiang and other members of the Gang of Four are arrested shortly after his death.

1976–1980: Gang of Four in prison; CCP conducts smear campaign with millions of posters and cartoons depicting Jiang as an empress, prostitute, and finally, "the white-boned demon."

1980–81: Gang of Four members tried and convicted of "counter-revolutionary crimes" in televised sensational trial; Jiang infamously says in her defense, "I was Chairman Mao's dog. Whomever he told me to bite, I bit." After initial death sentences, their sentences are commuted to life imprisonment.

1991: Jiang dies by suicide.